CHRISTMA

NOR

Kipper Williams

AMBERLEY

A number of these cartoons originally appeared in the Guardian, *the* Spectator, *the* Sunday Times, Private Eye, Country Life *or* Recharge, *so thanks to all concerned for allowing them to be used again here. Thanks also to* E&T *magazine for permission to reuse the cartoons on pages 4 and 14.*
Cartoons on pages 7, 15, 27 and 45 © Paperlink 2016.

First published 2016

Amberley Publishing
The Hill, Stroud,
Gloucestershire, GL5 4EP
www.amberley-books.com

ISBN 978 1 4456 6366 1 (print)
ISBN 978 1 4456 6367 8 (ebook)

British Library Cataloguing in Publication Data.
A catalogue record for this book is available from the British Library.

Typesetting and Origination by Amberley Publishing.
Printed in the UK.

Kipper Williams

SHALL I CARVE?
LIGHT SABER
Kipper Williams

CHRISTMAS TRUCE
Kipper Williams

HANG ON — THAT'S A FOSSIL FUEL!
Kipper Williams

RUN-UP
TO
CHRISTMAS
Kipper Williams

ACCORDING TO OUR IDENTITY CHECKS, YOU DON'T EXIST
CV
KipperWilliams

GOLD! WOW!
IT WAS TRADING AT AROUND $870 THIS WEEK – BUT SOME SAY IT'LL CLIMB TO $2,000 AN OUNCE ...
AT THIS RATE WE'LL BE ABLE TO AFFORD A HOTEL

Kipper Williams

A STILTON IS FOR LIFE AND NOT JUST FOR CHRISTMAS
Kipper Williams

BANKERS' BONUSES
£
Kipper Williams

London
STOCK
EXCHANGE
Kipper Williams

NEW
Christmas
Gadgets
THIS ONE ALERTS YOU TO ALL THE NEW CHRISTMAS GADGETS
KipperWilliams

IT'S ONLY 27 DAYS TO CHRISTMAS, SO YOUR MOTHER'S COME TO PUT THE SPROUTS ON
Kipper Williams

Kipperwilliams
CHARGING POINT

Kipper Williams

I come here to escape the mild British winters
South Pole
Kipper Williams

BRIBERY
PROBE
for
Santa

JUST WHAT I WANTED
KipperWilliams

Landfill
HE'S CUTTING OUT THE MIDDLE MAN
KipperWilliams

SOAP Powder
Snowman's Weekly
KW

NOW WILL YOU BELIEVE IN CLIMATE CHANGE?
Kipper Williams

King Wenceslas
Residence
FEAST of STEPHEN
I'M GOOD
KipperWilliams

Kipper Williams

Gallery of
SURREALISM
Kipper
Williams

PANETTONE
Panettone
PANETTONE
Kipper Williams

BETHLEHEM
Little Town
N93
SILENT NIGHT BUS
KipperWilliams

'Across the field, left at the fountain,
over the moor and right at the mountain.'

TURKEY FARM
WE'RE ALL IN THIS TOGETHER
Kipper Williams

Christmas Gifts
2nd: STUFF YOU'VE ALREADY GOT
1st: STUFF YOU DON'T REALLY NEED
Gnd: STUFF YOU DON'T REALLY WANT
Kipper Williams

olly Snowman
BAR
KipperWilliams

THE JUMPER'S TO WARD OFF EVIL SPIRITS
Ancient Yuletide Customs

'Stuffing . . . stuffing . . .'

Bank
Kipper Williams

FREE RANGE
MINCE
PIES

KipperWilliams

YOU'RE IMPOSSIBLE TO BUY FOR
Christmas Gift Ideas
Kipper Williams

NUDE
CHARITY
CALENDAR
Kipper
Williams

Christmas
WINE CLUB
KipperWilliams

Either my stomach's rumbling or they've started fracking
Kipper Williams

DEITY
ON
BOARD
Kipper
Williams

It came in handy for trussing up the turkey
Lingerie Rouge
KW

LAST YEAR WE WENT TO THEM, SO THIS YEAR THEY'RE COMING TO US.
Kipper Williams

BLOW YOUR CARROT!
Kipper Williams

BIRD FLU
ACHOO!

Winter Olympics
Kipper Williams

BAR HUMBUG
Resi
CHRISTMAS OPENING TIMES
Dec 21-Jan 5 CLOSED
KipperWilliams

QUOTAS FOR WOMEN
KipperWilliams

STOP
BOB BOB BOB
Kipper Williams

'This year I'll be heading somewhere hot.'

WHO LIKES CHARADES?

Planet News
EARTH ENTERS ICE AGE
KipperWilliams

LOOK OUT
— HE'S GOT A
CARROT!
Kipper Williams

CLOSED
FOR
CHRISTMAS
DYSFUNCTION
KW

Kipper Williams

HOME
ALONE
Kipper
Williams

THAT'S TERRIBLY INTERESTING. NOW LET ME TELL YOU ABOUT MY DEFAULT BROWSER
Micro soft

'Michelangelo, when I asked you to carve...'

LIFE IS A DOG
AND NOT JUST
FOR CHRISTMAS

Strictly Come
Prancing
Kipper
Williams

LITTLE TOWN OF BETHLEHEM SAYS NO TO VASTCO SUPERSTORE
Kipper Williams

AND NOW, THE END IS NEAR ...
Kipper Williams